The Amazing Adventures of Super Bear

Make every adventure amazing! Jorie M·

Fulton Books, Inc.
Meadville, PA

Published by Fulton Books 2020

ISBN 978-1-64952-312-9 (paperback)
ISBN 978-1-64952-313-6 (digital)

Printed in the United States of America

The Amazing Adventures of Super Bear

Super Bear Helps a Town

Lanie Melvin

Introduction

Born out of a lack of stuffed animals to display in her window for the Great New Hampshire Bear Hunt, but a desire to participate, Lanie created Super Bear.

The Great NH Bear Hunt was a Facebook group that contained a map. People would put a stuffed animal inside or outside their houses and log their city or town and their street. Families would then go "hunt" for the stuffed animals. It was a socially distanced activity for everyone during the "stay at home" order.

Every day from April 29, 2020, to May 24, 2020, Lanie created a different bear with a different take on the COVID-19 outbreak and stay-at-home orders. To date, there have been thirty-four different bear personalities, from a doctor/nurse bear to a librarian bear to a city worker bear and everything in between.

CUB SCHOOL

Bakery

Everything had come to a stop.
No cubs on the playground hop, hop, hop.
No sounds from the restaurant chop, chop, chop.
No bears in the stores to shop, shop, shop.

Super Bear saw with his own eyes.
There was no one around; it was such a surprise.
It was like a big top game without a prize
Or like a burger without the fries
Or a bakery without the pies.
No, it was more like raindrops from sunny skies.

This sickness has every bear staying home,
From the USA all the way to Rome.

"Where shall I start?"
"Is it with the bear at the mart, that one with the cart?"
No! In a town with such trouble, I'll have to be smart! Super Bear thought.

TEDDY GROCERY

HOSPITAL

Super Bear flew around the town looking for bears in trouble.
It wasn't long before he saw a bear carrying a bundle.
"Doctor Bear, that looks like a lot to juggle!" Super Bear exclaimed.
"These supplies are needed at the hospital fast, like, on the double.
With all the bears getting sick, it has become
a struggle," answered Doctor Bear.
"We got the call our packages were ready, but
Trucker Bear said he had too many!"
"We had no supplies, our cabinets were empty, but with this
package, we should now have plenty!" Doctor Bear explained.
"Trucker Bear is never late with his delivery. He must be
overloaded and way too busy," said Super Bear.

Super Bear flew to the city where Trucker
Bear was in a tizzy and Warehouse
Bear was making everyone dizzy.

GOODS
do not delay

"All of my coworkers are sick."
"I need some help real quick!" said Warehouse Bear.
Super Bear thought for a moment, *If I can find*
Warehouse Bear some help, that would surely do the trick.
"I will find you some help, Warehouse Bear,
someone to be your sidekick," Super Bear said.
"Finding help might be hard. I will have to look
in the streets, in the homes, and in the yards."

If I can find help, it will get Trucker Bear moving
faster, and then we can certainly avoid a shipping
disaster, Super Bear said to himself.

6

Just then, he saw a bear that was looking pretty down.
"Hey there, Business Bear, why do you wear
such a frown?" asked Super Bear.
"I have lost my job, the one downtown.
I want to offer my help, but there's no one around," said Business Bear.
"Well, you're in luck, you'll never guess what I have found!"
And soon Business Bear was warehouse-bound.

It wasn't long before he knew, Super
Bear was called to the rescue.
It was Restaurant Bear and his crew.
"Super Bear, we're so thankful it is you.
My restaurant is shut down, and we don't know what to do."

Restaurant

closed

"Most restaurants are starting to deliver, I have heard,
And I must admit, my curiosity has been stirred.
I need all the bears who know how to cook and
all the bears who know how to serve.
Asking them to deliver? Well, that's just absurd," said Restaurant Bear.
"I will find you some help. A bear with skills that can be transferred,"
Super Bear said as he buzzed away like a hummingbird.

It wasn't long before he knew.
There was a bear in need of help, but what did this bear do?
Super Bear hadn't a clue.

"Just a week ago, my business was thriving.
But now the schools are closed and no one is attending,
And the airport is empty, so no one is arriving!
I should be on the road driving!" said Bus Driver Bear.

TRANSPORT

"I have a thought. I know a bear that has an open spot. You would be perfect for this slot. This experience I know you've got. Do you want to give it a shot?" Super Bear asked. Bus Driver Bear nodded yes and drove out of the parking lot. *Bus Driver Bear will be perfect for Restaurant Bear's open slot*, Super Bear thought.

Just then, Super Bear bumped into Grocer Bear.
"Grocer Bear, are you okay? You look all frazzled," Super Bear asked.
"My store is in shambles, and it has me a bit rattled."

"My shelves are usually stocked to the
brim, but now it looks pretty grim.
Bears are panicking, and my stock is wearing thin.

All the stores are like this no matter where I have been. I need help, Super Bear. I need more bear women and more bear men," Grocer Bear explained. Super Bear thought for a moment, and the answer came to him. "I will find you some help, Grocer Bear, and don't worry, things will be normal again." Super Bear thought, *I don't know how many bears are needed. Could be one, but maybe ten!*

14

Super Bear could not believe what he saw just then.
It was the town's Bear Librarian.
"Librarian Bear, I have never seen you without
a grin!" Super Bear said kindly.
"They closed the schools and now the library. What about all the children?
I know things will get better, but my patience is wearing thin.
Where will I go? I want to help, but where do I begin?"

"How about having an online children's story group.
You could read about all different things.
One day all about animals from the cutest furry four-
legged to the scariest ones with fins.
And another day all about how dinosaurs that walked
the earth and how many years it has been.
There are so many children's books. You could
really have fun," Super Bear suggested.
"What a great idea, Super Bear. I'm going to do that right now. Bye,
Super Bear. I gotta run!" said Librarian Bear as she scooted off.

Super Bear soared into the sky; it
was just beyond the Grocer's store.
He saw a bear crying, but
he didn't know what for.
"Baker Bear, what is the matter?
You look as though your heart is
pretty sore," asked Super Bear.
"There are no bears buying
my pastries, so now I am
forced to close my store.
What am I going to do when I
close my door?" Baker Bear roared.
"Grocer Bear needs help. He will
tell you what for," Super Bear said.
So Baker Bear rushed along
to the grocery store.

Bread
of the
Day

17

Super Bear flew over to the school.
"Teacher Bear, how goes it?" asked Super Bear.
"Times are troubling, I have to admit.
Students are learning online to get their credit.
Teaching online is good, but it leaves out all the spirit.
Parents are working from home and
need someone to babysit.
I am just not sure who would be the best
fit," Teacher Bear explained.
"I have an idea, so I will send someone their way, and
don't worry, she will be a hit!" Super Bear said.

20

Super Bear flew over to his bear friend's house.
Everything was quiet over there, quiet as a mouse.
"I wonder where everyone could be?
I rang the doorbell, ring 1, ring 2, ring 3.
The doors are open. The lights are on. Surely
they know it's me!" wondered Super Bear.
Just then, a bear appeared in the doorway.
"College Bear, I know you are home, because
some bears at school have the sickness.
With all the parents and kids being
home like you, something is amiss.
I have an opportunity for you,
something you can't dismiss.
The parents are working, and the kids are restless.
The kids need someone fun to watch them.
Do you want to try this?" Super Bear said.
"That sounds like a ton of fun. How could
I resist?" College Bear answered.
"Stop at the school and talk to Teacher Bear.
I am sure she has a list," Super Bear said.

22

It was at the end of the day,
and Super Bear was tired.
He had helped a lot of bears
who needed to be hired.

Just as he was about to take flight,
He saw something behind him, a red-and-blue light.
"Hello, Police Officer Bear, how is your night?" Super Bear asked.
"I need you to follow me back to the station. You won't
believe the sight," Police Officer Bear answered.

Police Station

As they arrived at the station, Super
Bear couldn't believe his eyes.
All the bears in town greeted him with their cries.
"Hip hip HOOORAY, hip hip HOOORAY!" they all
screamed for him; it was such a surprise.
Super Bear got to the stage, and he
could feel his heart start to rise.

Firefighter Bear came to the stage too.
"From all of us, we want to thank you.
You have done so much for so many.
We weren't sure if you knew.
By telling College Bear of the need for a
sitter, that family's company grew.
By sharing the need for a delivery crew,
Restaurant Bear created something new.
By finding help for Warehouse Bear, Trucker Bear
made his deliveries. Now he only has a few.
By finding help for Grocer Bear, his store
is stocked all the way through."

Super Bear started to speak when he got the cue.
"What you don't know is, this
is because of all of you.
You all pitched in to lend a hand
and become part of the crew.
So this honor belongs to all of us, not
just me, you too!" yelled Super Bear.

As Super Bear looked around, he could see with his own eyes,
Maybe now the bakery will have some pies, and
maybe all the burgers will come with fries?
And the good thing about raindrops from sunny
skies is, there is always a rainbow surprise.
The cubs were back on the playground hop-hop-hopping.
The sounds were joyously coming from the
restaurant chop-chop-chopping.

As Super Bear flew away,
He thought he heard a bear say,
"If you are not willing to chip in and help,
Then no matter how far or how high Super Bear flies,
You will never ever get that big top prize."

TEDDY GROCERY

HOSPITAL

Super bear was so proud
of this little town.
They all pitched in to help
one another, and now this
is the best town around.

The End

About the Author

Lanie Melvin grew up the older of two children, in a suburb town north of Boston, Massachusetts. Eventually, she relocated to southern New Hampshire, which is where she resides with her husband and dogs today. *The Amazing Adventures of Super Bear: Super Bear Helps a Town* is Lanie's first publication, but additional books in the *Super Bear Adventures* are already in the works. Though she has no children of her own, her children by marriage have blessed her with two granddaughters and a grandson. Lanie's younger sibling has blessed her with two nephews as well. She enjoys playing with her dogs, doing crafts of all kinds, including a line of "bear hug cards" that she designs and hand-makes to order, volunteering for animal rescues, playing with her grandchildren and nephews, and of course, she loves to write children's stories.

CPSIA information can be obtained
at www.ICGtesting.com
Printed in the USA
JSHW040025160321
12552JS00002B/3